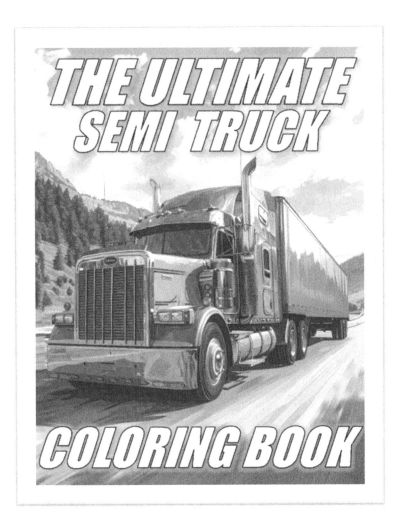

MW01168909

and want more fun, be sure to check out our website or find us on Amazon search for:

Coco Bean Coloring Books

WWW. COCOBEANPUBLISHING. COM

## The Ultimate Semi Truck Coloring Book
ISBN: 979-8874352738

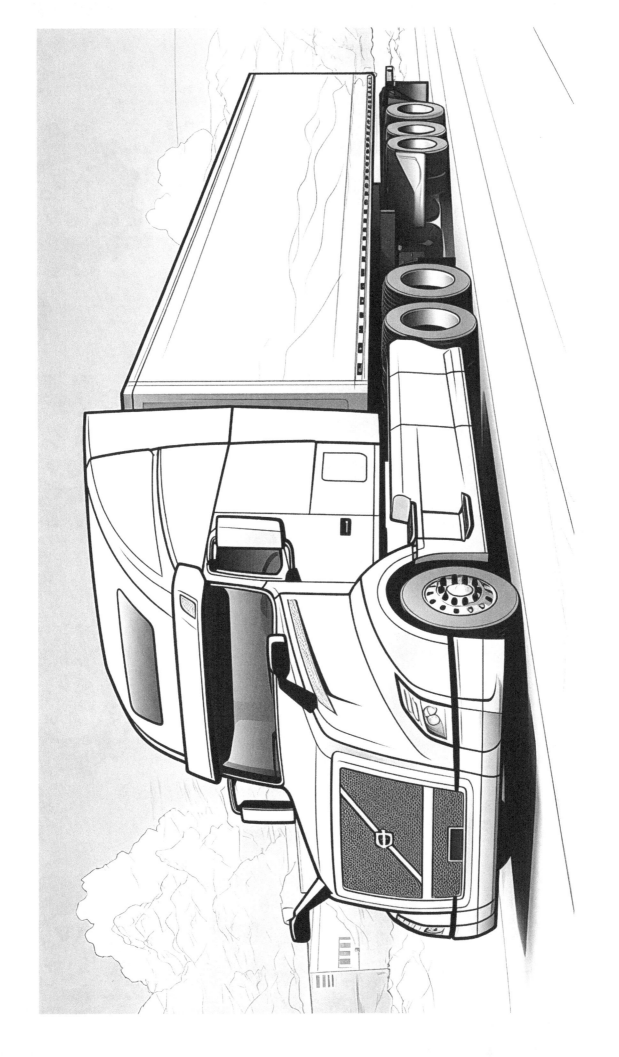

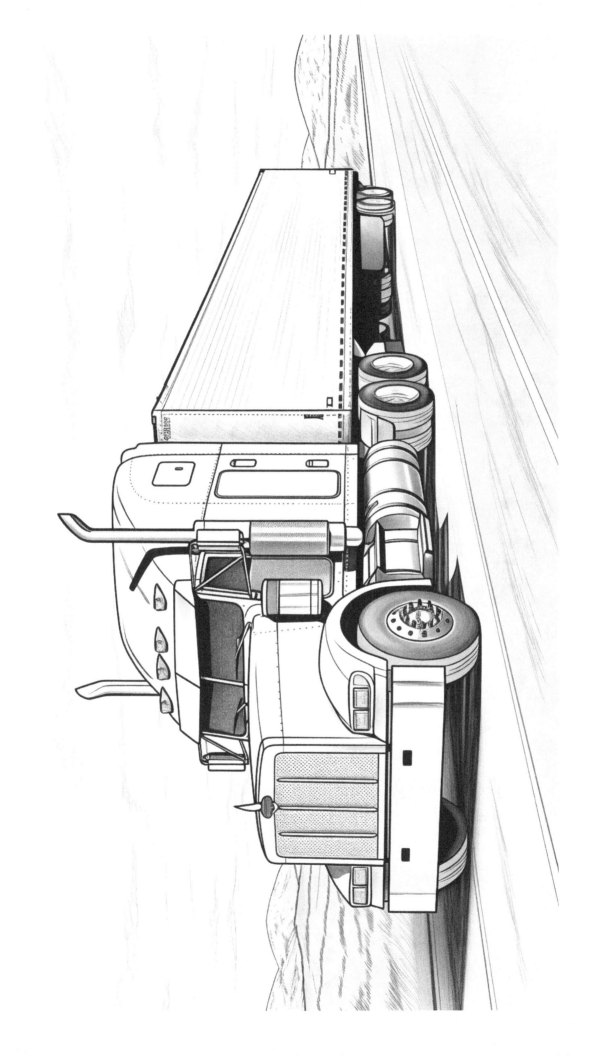

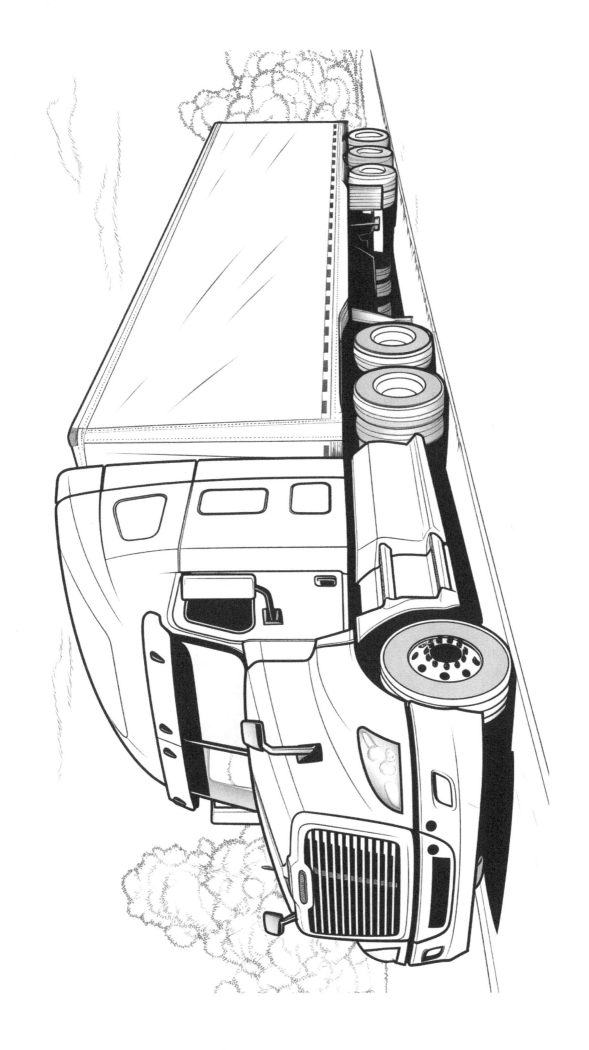

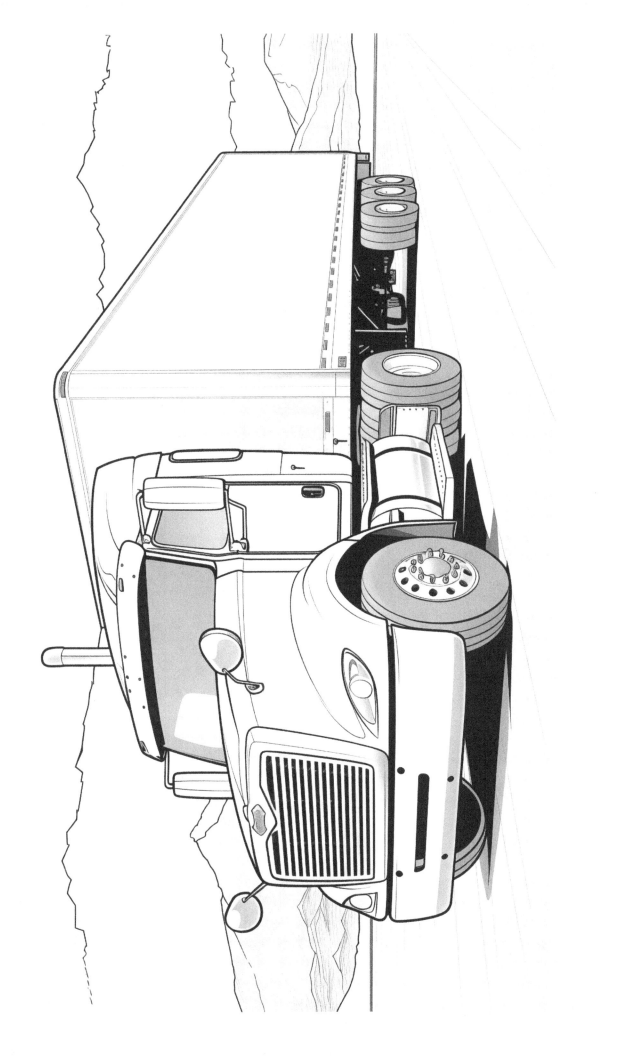

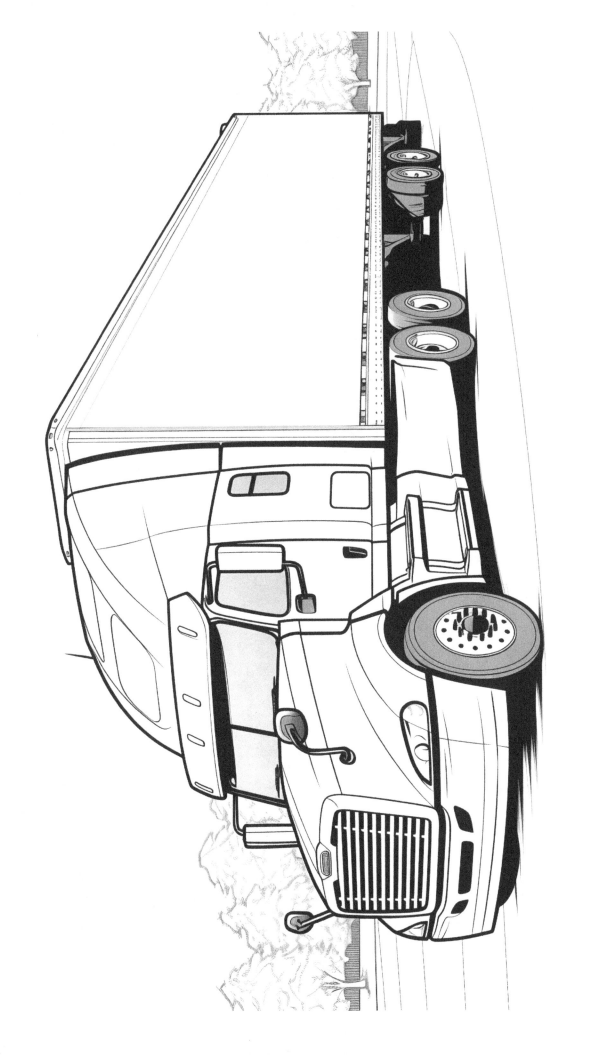

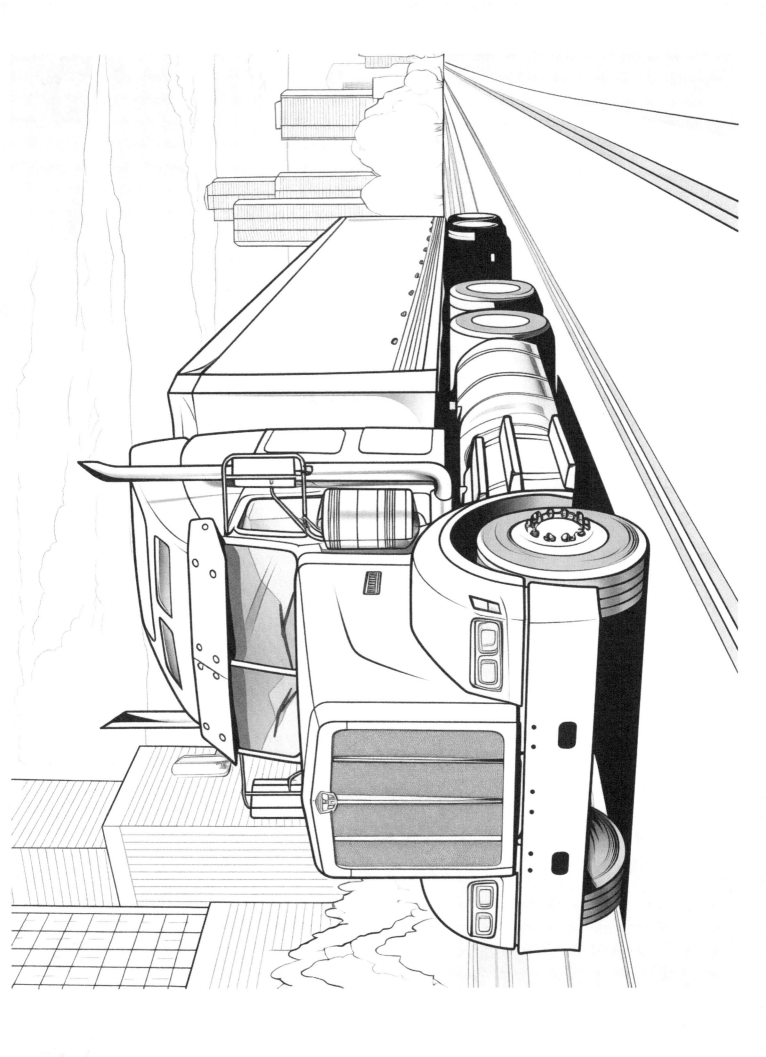

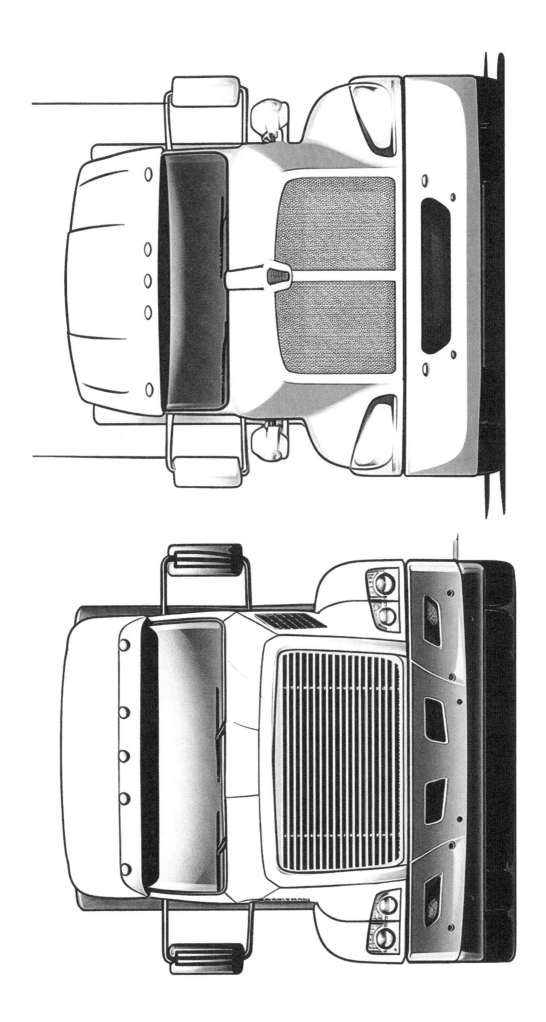

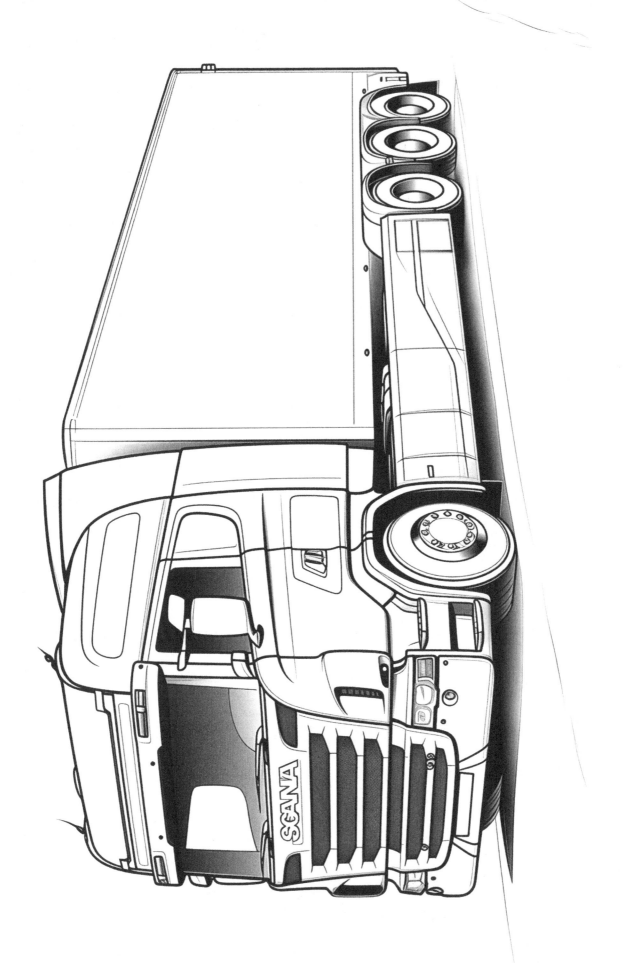

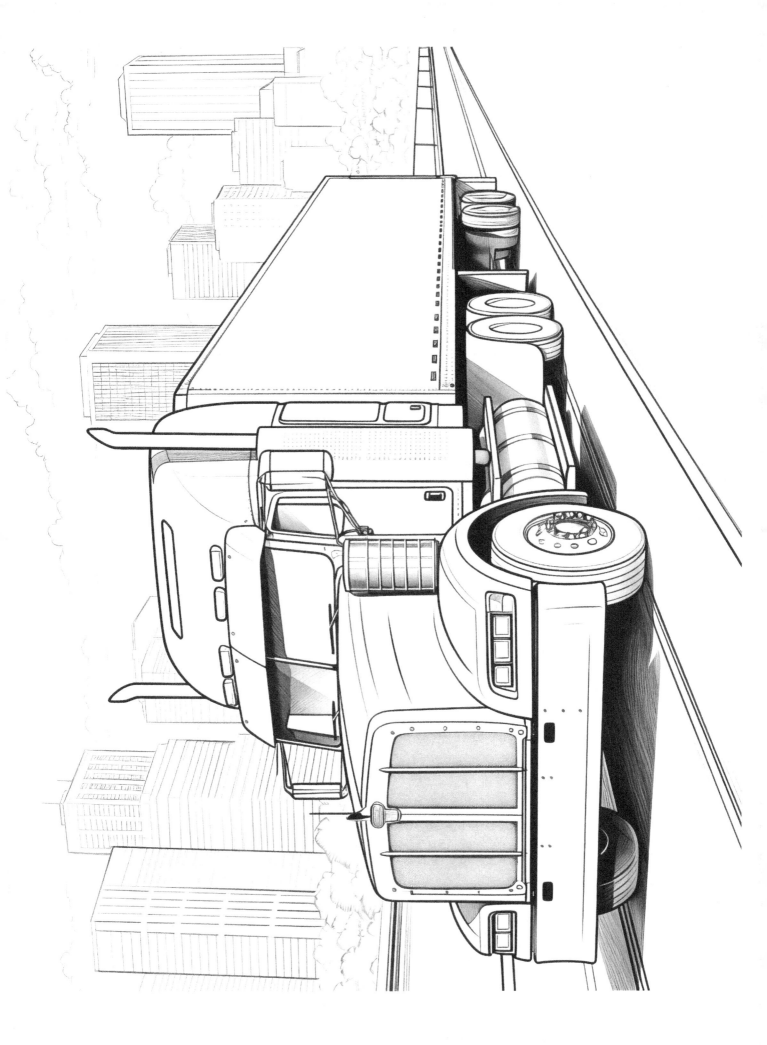

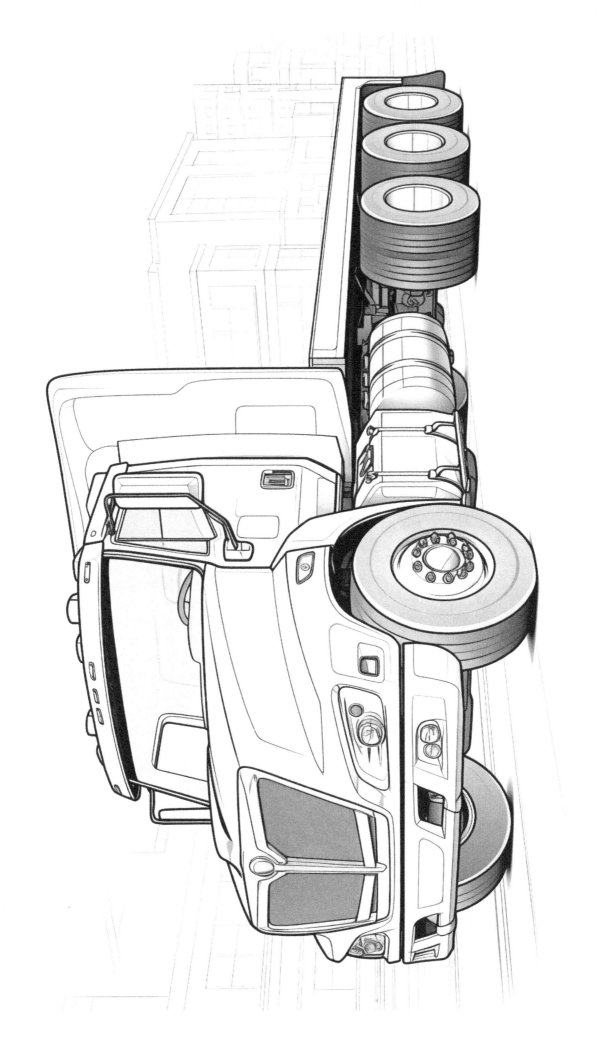

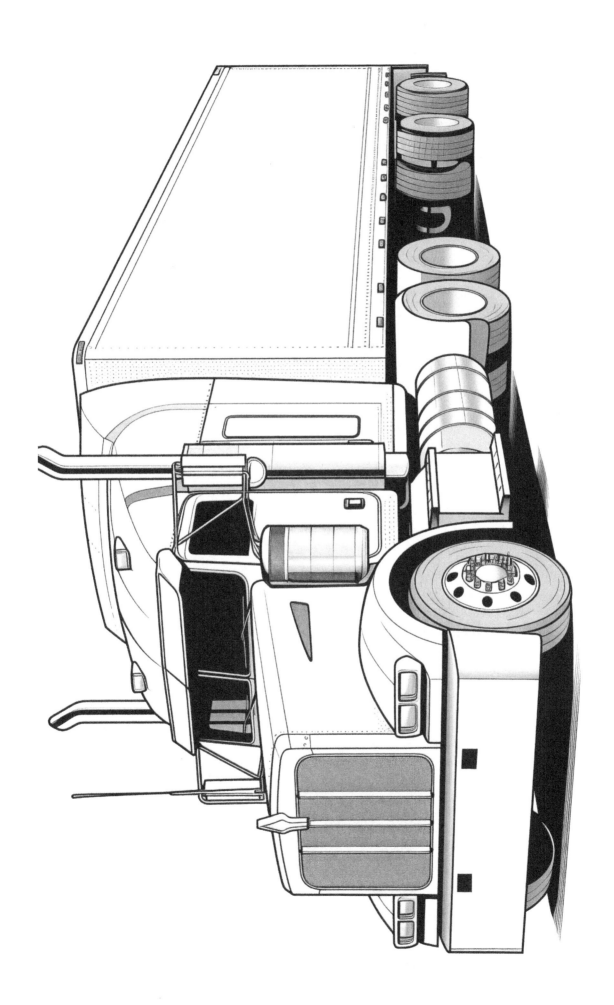

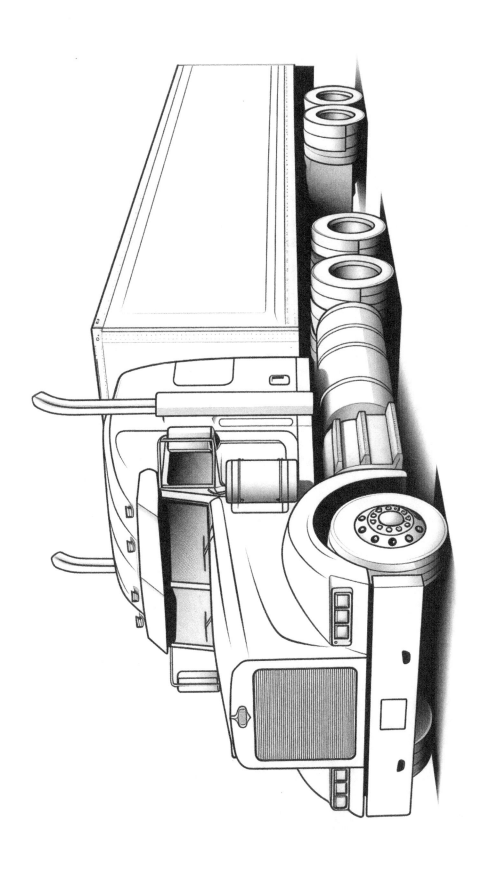

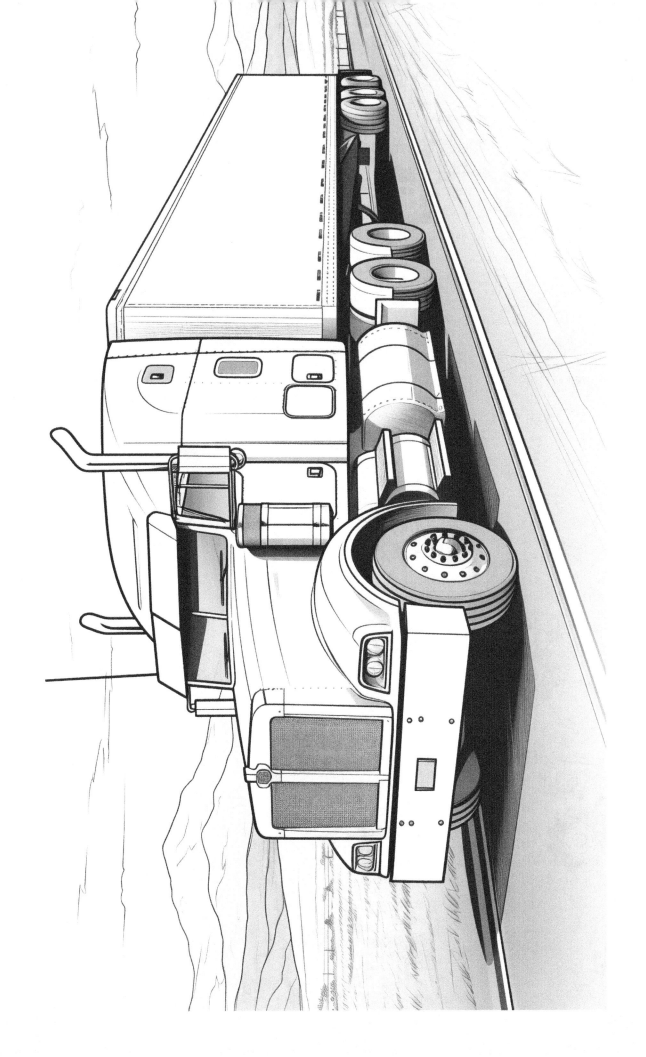

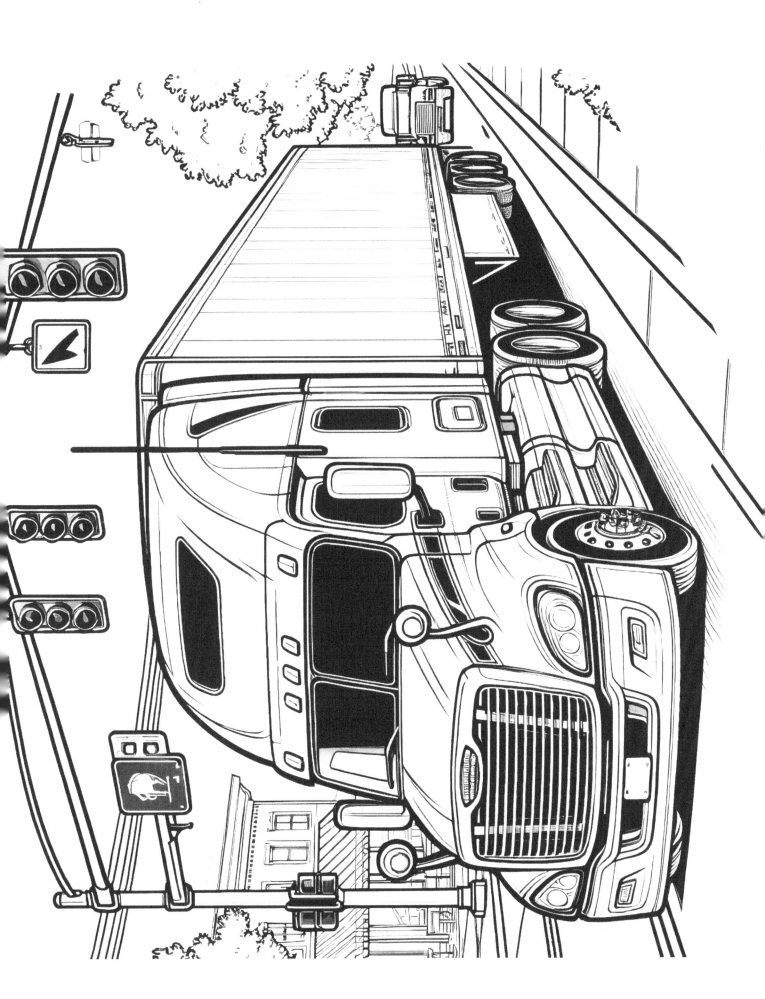

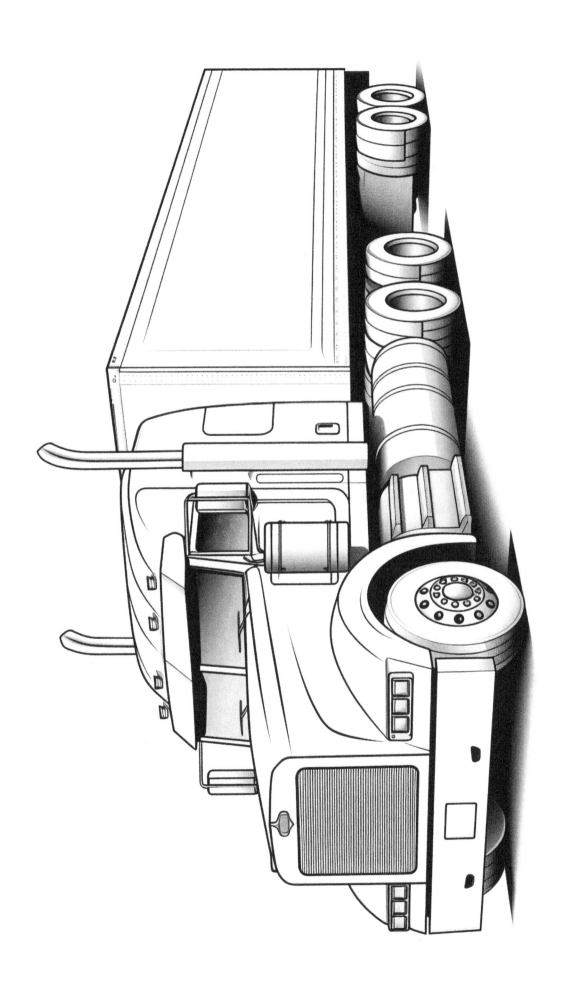

**Dinosaur Dreamland**
*A Dino Coloring Book*
ISBN: 979-8395084422

# BONUS COLORING PAGE

**A Cat's Meow Kingdom**
*A Cat Coloring Book*
ISBN: 979-8395297747

# BONUS COLORING PAGE

Made in the USA
Monee, IL
05 December 2024

72626764R00057